Glen Powell The Rise of Hollywood's Charismatic Leading Man

From Small Town Dreams to Blockbuster Success Exploring His Journey, Impact and Legacy in Film and Beyond

Beatrice G. George

Copyright © Beatrice G. George 2024

No part of this publication may be reproduced, distributed, or transmitted in any form or by any means, including photocopying, recording, or other electronic or mechanical methods, without the prior written permission of the publisher, except in the case of brief quotations embodied in critical reviews and certain other noncommercial uses permitted by copyright law.

Table Of Contents

Introduction

Chapter 1: Early Life
Birth and Family Background
Childhood Experiences and Early Interests in Performing Arts
Community Support and Early Recognition

Chapter 2: Education
High School Achievements and Extracurricular Activities
College Education at the University of Texas at Austin
A Balancing Act of Dreams and Reality

Chapter 3: Career Beginnings
Initial Roles in Film and Television
Navigating Challenges and Staying Persistent

Chapter 4: Rising Fame
Soaring with Top Gun: Maverick
Contributions as a Writer and Producer
Balanced Approach to Stardom

Chapter 5: Personal Life
Relationships and Significant Personal Experiences
Lifestyle and Hobbies
Balancing Fame and Privacy
Insights into His Personalit

Chapter 6: Net Worth
Financial Success in Hollywood
Earnings as a Writer and Producer

Chapter 7: Legacy and Impact
Influence on the Film Industry
Recognition in Awards and Honors
Looking to the Future

Chapter 8: Professional Skills
Mastery of Acting

Talent as a Writer
The Future of Powell's Career

Conclusion

Introduction

Glen Powell is a name that resonates with charm, talent, and versatility in Hollywood. Over the past decade, he has steadily risen from supporting roles to a formidable presence in the entertainment industry, captivating audiences with his magnetic performances.

Known for his wide smile and natural charisma, Powell has built a reputation for embodying dynamic and relatable characters, making him one of the most promising actors of his generation. Born and raised in Texas, Powell's ascent to stardom is a testament to hard work, ambition, and an unshakable passion for storytelling. Whether he's portraying a cocky fighter pilot, a determined mathematician, or a love-struck romantic, his performances consistently leave a lasting impression. From the early days of his career, Powell demonstrated an unwavering dedication to honing his craft, which ultimately led to standout roles that have solidified his place in the film world.

His breakout moment came with his role in Scream Queens, a horror-comedy series that allowed Powell to showcase his comedic timing and dramatic flair. However, it was his portrayal of the confident yet endearing aviator "Hangman" in Top Gun: Maverick that catapulted him into global recognition.

The film's massive success not only broke box office records but also highlighted Powell's ability to hold his own alongside seasoned stars like Tom Cruise. Beyond acting, Powell's talents extend to writing and producing, showcasing his multifaceted contribution to the creative process. His efforts behind the camera are a reflection of his commitment to exploring new dimensions of storytelling, proving he's more than just a leading man. This dedication to creativity has made him a well-rounded artist with a bright future ahead. In addition to his professional achievements, Powell has cultivated a genuine connection with his fans.

Off-screen, he is admired for his down-to-earth personality and active engagement with charitable causes. Whether supporting veterans or advocating for mental health awareness, Powell's efforts reflect his desire to use his platform for good. This biography delves into the life and journey of Glen Powell, exploring his Texas roots, academic pursuits, and the pivotal moments that shaped his flourishing career.

From his first on-screen appearances to the blockbuster hits that cemented his status as a Hollywood star, Powell's story is one of determination, talent, and an undeniable passion for his craft. As we trace his rise to fame, we'll uncover the personal and professional experiences that have defined him, shedding light on the man behind the roles. Glen Powell is not just a performer; he's a storyteller, a dreamer, and a figure of inspiration for aspiring artists everywhere.

Chapter 1: Early Life

Birth and Family Background

Glen Powell was born on October 21, 1988, in Austin, Texas, a city known for its vibrant arts culture and deep-rooted traditions. Coming from a family that valued hard work and creativity, Powell grew up in an environment that encouraged him to dream big. His parents, Cyndy and Glen Sr., were supportive figures who played an instrumental role in shaping his ambitions.

Glen, the middle child, shared his childhood with two sisters, Lauren and Leslie, both of whom were his early confidants and cheerleaders. Growing up in a household filled with love, laughter, and a dash of mischief, Powell experienced a quintessential Texan upbringing. His father, a man with a sharp sense of humor, often shared stories that sparked young Glen's imagination. His mother, on the other hand, instilled in him the values of empathy and resilience, traits that would later become integral to his success in the cutthroat world of Hollywood.

Childhood Experiences and Early Interests in Performing Arts

Powell's childhood was anything but ordinary. From a young age, he exhibited an infectious energy and a natural flair for entertaining those around him. Whether it was performing impromptu skits for his family or imitating characters he saw on TV, Powell had an undeniable knack for the spotlight. His early years were marked by a mix of playful antics and a budding interest in storytelling.

Austin's vibrant cultural scene also played a pivotal role in nurturing Powell's creative side. Frequent visits to local theaters and outdoor performances left a lasting impression on him. Inspired by the performers he watched, Powell began dreaming of a life where he could tell stories that moved audiences. His curiosity about acting was further piqued when he attended his first live stage production—a memory he often described as a defining moment in his decision to pursue a career in the performing arts. However, it wasn't just acting that captured Powell's attention during his formative years.

He was also drawn to athletics, music, and academics. As a young boy, he dabbled in sports, particularly football, a passion shared by many Texans. But despite his love for the game, his heart always leaned toward creative pursuits. Powell's first brush with the entertainment industry came in an unexpected way. At the age of 10, he was cast as an extra in a small community theater production.

While the role itself was minor, the experience ignited something profound within him. The thrill of being part of a collaborative creative process was exhilarating, and it left Powell wanting more. His ambitions became even clearer during his teenage years when he began exploring film as a medium. Equipped with a camcorder gifted by his parents, Powell would gather his friends and siblings to create short films. These homemade projects, though amateur, were a reflection of his burgeoning talent and unyielding passion for storytelling. One particular short film, which he humorously titled The Adventures of Glen & Friends, showcased his ability to direct, act, and entertain all at once.

Though the production quality was far from polished, it demonstrated his knack for crafting compelling narratives—a skill he would later refine in Hollywood.

Community Support and Early Recognition

Powell's early ventures into acting did not go unnoticed. His local community took pride in his talents, often encouraging him to participate in school plays and neighborhood talent shows. Teachers and mentors recognized his potential early on, describing him as a student who possessed both natural talent and a remarkable work ethic. One of his most memorable performances during this time was in a middle school production of Peter Pan, where Powell played the mischievous title character. His portrayal of the boy who never grows up left his peers and teachers in awe, cementing his reputation as a gifted performer. The experience also solidified Powell's desire to pursue acting more seriously, as he realized the impact a well-told story could have on an audience.

Despite his early successes, Powell's journey wasn't without its challenges. Growing up in a city like Austin, where creativity thrived, meant competing with many talented peers. There were moments of self-doubt, especially when roles didn't come his way or when his work wasn't recognized as much as he had hoped. Yet, these obstacles only fueled his determination. Powell credits his family for keeping him grounded during these formative years.

Their unwavering belief in his potential gave him the confidence to push through setbacks and continue pursuing his dreams. By the time Powell reached his teenage years, he had already laid a solid foundation for what would become a remarkable career. His experiences growing up in Austin provided him with a unique perspective on storytelling—one that valued authenticity and creativity above all else. The combination of a supportive family, a culturally rich upbringing, and an unrelenting drive to succeed shaped Powell into the artist he is today. His early life wasn't just a precursor to fame; it was the bedrock upon which his future achievements were built.

Chapter 2: Education

High School Achievements and Extracurricular Activities

Glen Powell's educational journey began at Westwood High School in Austin, Texas, where he quickly distinguished himself as a well-rounded student. Known for his affable personality and infectious energy, Powell was a natural leader among his peers.

He was not only academically inclined but also actively involved in a variety of extracurricular activities, which provided him with the foundation for his future success. Powell excelled in academics, maintaining impressive grades that reflected his dedication to learning. His teachers often noted his inquisitive nature and ability to think creatively, qualities that would later serve him well as an actor and storyteller. Beyond academics, Powell embraced the opportunities his school offered in sports, arts, and leadership roles. Athletically, Powell had a particular passion for football, a sport that held immense cultural significance in Texas.

As a member of the school's team, he demonstrated discipline, teamwork, and perseverance, traits that would later influence his professional approach to acting and filmmaking. However, while he enjoyed the camaraderie of sports, his true passion lay in the arts. Powell's involvement in theater was pivotal during his high school years.

Participating in school plays and drama competitions allowed him to refine his craft and build confidence as a performer. One of his standout performances was in a production of Our Town, where his portrayal of a central character earned widespread praise. His natural ability to connect with an audience became evident, and it was clear that acting wasn't just a hobby—it was his calling. In addition to theater, Powell was an active participant in student government and various clubs. His leadership skills shone as he organized events and rallied his classmates around creative projects. These experiences not only enhanced his public speaking abilities but also gave him a sense of responsibility and purpose.

College Education at the University of Texas at Austin

After graduating from high school, Powell decided to stay close to his roots by attending the University of Texas at Austin (UT Austin). The decision was both practical and sentimental, as UT Austin is known for its exceptional programs in film and arts, aligning perfectly with Powell's aspirations.

Enrolling in the Moody College of Communication, Powell immersed himself in the study of film, communication, and the performing arts. His time at UT Austin was transformative, providing him with the technical knowledge and creative inspiration he needed to pursue a career in Hollywood. One of the highlights of his college experience was his involvement in the Texas Student Television network, where he collaborated with like-minded peers to create original content. These projects allowed Powell to experiment with writing, directing, and acting, honing his skills in a hands-on environment.

Whether working behind the camera or in front of it, Powell demonstrated a relentless drive to learn and improve. Balancing academics with his passion for acting wasn't always easy. Powell frequently traveled between Austin and Los Angeles for auditions and acting opportunities, a demanding routine that required exceptional time management and determination. Despite the challenges, he managed to maintain his focus, excelling both as a student and as an aspiring actor.

UT Austin also provided Powell with invaluable networking opportunities. The university's vibrant arts community introduced him to mentors and collaborators who would play crucial roles in his career. It was during this time that Powell began to make inroads into the entertainment industry, landing small roles in films and TV shows. One notable opportunity came when Powell was cast in The Great Debaters (2007), a critically acclaimed film directed by Denzel Washington. Although his role was minor, the experience of working alongside industry veterans was a turning point. It reaffirmed his commitment to pursuing acting as a lifelong career and gave him a taste of the professional world he aspired to be part of.

A Balancing Act of Dreams and Reality

Powell's college years were marked by a delicate balance between pursuing his Hollywood dreams and fulfilling his academic responsibilities. This dual pursuit was not without its sacrifices. There were late nights spent studying for exams after returning from auditions, and moments of self-doubt when rejection threatened to derail his confidence. Yet, Powell's resilience kept him moving forward.

His parents and professors remained steadfast sources of support during this time. They encouraged him to stay the course, reminding him that every setback was a stepping stone to something greater. This unwavering belief in his potential gave Powell the courage to persevere, even when the odds seemed stacked against him. By the time Powell graduated from UT Austin, he had not only earned a degree but also gained a wealth of experience that would shape his future endeavors. His time at the university taught him the importance of collaboration, adaptability, and perseverance—lessons that would prove invaluable as he navigated the challenges of the entertainment industry.

Powell's college years were more than just an academic journey; they were a period of self-discovery and growth. The relationships he built, the projects he undertook, and the lessons he learned all contributed to the foundation of his success. As Powell prepared to leave Austin and embark on the next chapter of his life, he carried with him a deep appreciation for his roots and a determination to make his mark in Hollywood. Little did he know that his dreams were about to take flight in ways he had only imagined.

Chapter 3: Career Beginnings

Initial Roles in Film and Television

Glen Powell's first steps into the world of acting were humble but determined. Starting with minor roles, he quickly gained valuable experience that would later propel him into the spotlight. One of his earliest appearances was in the critically acclaimed film The Great Debaters (2007), where he shared the screen with Denzel Washington and Forest Whitaker.

Although his role was small, it was an essential stepping stone, exposing Powell to the rigors of professional acting and the dynamics of a high-profile production. Following this, Powell landed a series of small parts in television shows and movies, gradually building his résumé. His appearances in shows like Jack & Bobby and CSI: Miami showcased his ability to adapt to various genres, from drama to procedural crime stories. These early roles may not have been glamorous, but they were vital for sharpening his craft and introducing him to the mechanics of the industry. Despite the limited screen time, Powell's natural charisma and dedication to his roles didn't go unnoticed.

Casting directors appreciated his professionalism and his ability to bring depth to even the most minor characters. These early years were a testing ground, teaching Powell the importance of resilience and hard work in a competitive field. The turning point in Powell's career came with the Fox television series Scream Queens (2015-2016), created by Ryan Murphy, Brad Falchuk, and Ian Brennan. Powell was cast as Chad Radwell, a hilariously arrogant fraternity president whose comedic antics and over-the-top personality made him an instant fan favorite.

Powell's portrayal of Chad showcased his impeccable comedic timing and ability to fully commit to a character. The role allowed him to explore the absurd and satirical elements of his personality, proving that he could shine in comedy just as much as in drama. Critics praised Powell's performance, calling him one of the standout characters in the series. The success of Scream Queens gave Powell the visibility he needed to transition from supporting roles to more substantial opportunities. It also marked the first time he developed a significant fan base, with viewers appreciating his blend of humor, charm, and good looks.

More importantly, the role demonstrated Powell's range as an actor, setting him apart in an industry where versatility is key to longevity. During this period, Powell also began exploring creative avenues beyond acting. He expressed an interest in screenwriting and producing, planting the seeds for what would later become an essential aspect of his career. His time on Scream Queens not only boosted his confidence as an actor but also fueled his ambition to take on more multifaceted roles in the industry.

Navigating Challenges and Staying Persistent

While Scream Queens was a significant milestone, Powell's journey wasn't without its hurdles. Like many actors, he faced periods of uncertainty, auditioning for roles that didn't materialize and competing in an oversaturated market. However, Powell's perseverance and ability to maintain a positive outlook helped him navigate these challenges. He credits much of his resilience to the support of his family and friends, who consistently reminded him of his potential. These relationships provided a strong foundation during times when the unpredictability of the entertainment industry felt overwhelming.

Powell's unwavering belief in his craft and his willingness to embrace both successes and failures set him apart from many of his peers. As Powell continued to take on a variety of roles, he began to earn a reputation as one of Hollywood's most promising rising stars. Casting agents and directors appreciated his work ethic, adaptability, and collaborative spirit.

He was not only reliable on set but also brought a unique energy that elevated every project he was part of. During this phase, Powell started to strategically choose roles that aligned with his long-term career goals. Rather than taking on projects purely for exposure, he sought opportunities that allowed him to grow as an artist. This selective approach demonstrated a maturity and foresight uncommon in actors at the beginning of their careers. Powell's career beginnings were marked by meaningful collaborations with established actors and filmmakers. Working alongside seasoned professionals provided him with invaluable insights into the craft of acting and the intricacies of storytelling.

These experiences deepened his appreciation for the collaborative nature of filmmaking and inspired him to push his boundaries as a performer. One particularly memorable collaboration was with Richard Linklater, an acclaimed director known for his innovative approach to storytelling. Powell worked with Linklater on the film Everybody Wants Some!! (2016), a coming-of-age comedy that further showcased Powell's comedic abilities.

The movie was well-received by critics, with many praising Powell's performance as part of a talented ensemble cast. Powell also began forming connections with up-and-coming creators, recognizing the importance of nurturing relationships with peers who shared his passion for storytelling. These partnerships would later pave the way for Powell's ventures into writing and producing, allowing him to explore his creative vision beyond acting. By the end of this early phase of his career, Glen Powell had established himself as a versatile and committed actor with a bright future ahead. His journey from small roles to significant breakthroughs demonstrated his ability to adapt, persevere, and seize opportunities.

While the path to success was far from linear, Powell's dedication to his craft and his willingness to learn from every experience laid the groundwork for what was to come. As Powell moved into the next chapter of his career, he carried with him the lessons learned during these formative years. The challenges he faced and the victories he celebrated became stepping stones on his path to stardom, shaping him into the dynamic and multi-talented artist he is today.

Chapter 4: Rising Fame

Glen Powell's rise to prominence was cemented by his standout role as astronaut John Glenn in the critically acclaimed film Hidden Figures (2016). Directed by Theodore Melfi, the film tells the inspiring true story of three African American women whose mathematical expertise was instrumental to NASA's space program during the 1960s.

Powell's portrayal of John Glenn was both charismatic and heartfelt, embodying the charm and determination of the historic figure. His performance added depth to the ensemble cast, which included Taraji P. Henson, Octavia Spencer, and Janelle Monáe. Powell's ability to complement these powerhouse performances while leaving his unique mark on the film earned him widespread praise. The success of Hidden Figures went beyond critical acclaim. The film became a cultural phenomenon, shedding light on the overlooked contributions of women and minorities in STEM fields. For Powell, being part of such an impactful project was a defining moment in his career.

The movie's success solidified his reputation as a versatile actor capable of excelling in both dramatic and historical narratives.

Soaring with Top Gun: Maverick

In 2022, Powell reached new heights with his role in Top Gun: Maverick, the long-awaited sequel to the iconic 1986 film Top Gun. Directed by Joseph Kosinski, the film starred Tom Cruise, reprising his role as Pete "Maverick" Mitchell, and introduced a new generation of fighter pilots. Powell played Lieutenant Jake "Hangman" Seresin, a cocky yet skilled naval aviator whose competitive spirit often put him at odds with his fellow pilots. The role was a perfect fit for Powell, who brought a mix of swagger and vulnerability to the character. His performance added depth to Hangman, making him more than just an archetypal rival. The film's aerial sequences were a standout feature, with Powell and his co-stars undergoing rigorous training to perform realistic flight maneuvers. Powell's dedication to authenticity was evident, as he embraced the physical and mental challenges of portraying a fighter pilot.

His commitment paid off, with critics and audiences praising his performance as one of the film's highlights. Top Gun: Maverick was a massive box-office success, grossing over $1.4 billion worldwide and becoming one of the highest-grossing films of 2022. For Powell, the movie not only elevated his profile but also demonstrated his ability to thrive in blockbuster productions.

His role in the film marked a turning point, positioning him as one of Hollywood's most promising leading men. In 2024, Powell took on a new challenge with Anyone But You, a romantic comedy that showcased his ability to blend humor and heart. Co-starring Sydney Sweeney, the film followed two characters with a love-hate dynamic as they navigated an unexpected romance. Powell's charm and comedic timing were on full display in the film, which drew comparisons to classic rom-coms like When Harry Met Sally and The Proposal. His chemistry with Sweeney was a major draw, earning praise from critics and audiences alike. The movie's lighthearted tone and witty dialogue provided Powell with the opportunity to explore a different facet of his acting repertoire.

Anyone But You also marked Powell's increasing involvement in the creative process. As a producer on the project, he played a significant role in shaping the film's vision, from script development to casting decisions. This dual role as actor and producer highlighted Powell's growing influence in Hollywood and his commitment to telling engaging stories.

Contributions as a Writer and Producer

Beyond his on-screen performances, Powell has steadily built a reputation as a talented writer and producer. His creative ambitions were evident early in his career, but it was during his rise to fame that he began to take on more substantial behind-the-scenes roles. Powell co-wrote and co-produced Set It Up (2018), a Netflix romantic comedy that became a surprise hit. Starring Zoey Deutch and Glen Powell himself, the film reinvigorated the rom-com genre with its witty script and relatable characters. Powell's involvement in the project showcased his ability to craft stories that resonate with audiences, both as a writer and a performer.

In interviews, Powell has often spoken about his passion for storytelling and his desire to create meaningful content. His work as a producer reflects this ethos, with projects that balance entertainment value with substance. Whether developing scripts, collaborating with directors, or championing new talent, Powell's contributions to filmmaking extend far beyond his acting roles.

Balanced Approach to Stardom

As Powell's star continues to rise, he remains grounded in his approach to fame. He often credits his success to the people who supported him along the way, from his family and mentors to his collaborators in the industry. This humility, combined with his relentless drive, has endeared him to fans and colleagues alike. Powell's ability to navigate the complexities of Hollywood while staying true to his values has been a defining aspect of his career. He consistently chooses projects that align with his creative vision, prioritizing quality over quantity. This deliberate approach has allowed him to build a diverse and impressive body of work, earning him recognition as one of Hollywood's most dynamic talents.

With a string of successes under his belt, Powell is poised for even greater achievements. His ability to excel in both dramatic and comedic roles, coupled with his talent for storytelling, positions him as a true multi-hyphenate in the entertainment industry. As he continues to take on new challenges, Powell's commitment to growth and innovation ensures that his influence will only continue to expand. Whether starring in blockbuster films, producing compelling stories, or exploring new creative ventures, Glen Powell is undoubtedly a force to be reckoned with in Hollywood.

Chapter 5: Personal Life

Relationships and Significant Personal Experiences

Glen Powell's personal life has often been a topic of intrigue for his fans and the media. Known for his charm and affable personality, Powell has been linked to several high-profile relationships over the years. However, despite his rising fame, he has managed to maintain a level of privacy, keeping much of his personal life out of the public eye.

One of Powell's most notable relationships has been with Gigi Paris, a model and entrepreneur. The couple, often seen together at events and on social media, has shared glimpses of their relationship, showcasing their shared love for adventure and travel. Their chemistry and mutual support for each other's careers have made them a favorite among fans. Powell's connection with Paris reflects his grounded nature, as he values relationships that inspire and challenge him to grow. Powell's family also plays a significant role in his personal life. Despite his demanding career, he remains close to his parents and siblings, frequently expressing gratitude for their unwavering support.

Growing up in a tight-knit family instilled in Powell a strong sense of loyalty and resilience, qualities that have served him well in the unpredictable world of Hollywood.

Lifestyle and Hobbies

Outside of his work in the entertainment industry, Powell leads a vibrant and well-rounded lifestyle. An avid traveler, he enjoys exploring new cultures and immersing himself in different environments. His social media often features snapshots of his travels, from picturesque beaches to bustling cities, reflecting his adventurous spirit. Fitness is another cornerstone of Powell's lifestyle. Known for his athletic build, he often credits a disciplined workout routine and healthy eating habits for maintaining his physical and mental well-being. Whether preparing for a physically demanding role like in Top Gun: Maverick or simply enjoying outdoor activities like hiking and surfing, Powell's commitment to fitness is evident. One of Powell's lesser-known hobbies is his love for aviation.

Inspired by his work on Top Gun: Maverick, he has expressed an interest in learning to fly, showcasing his passion for pushing boundaries and exploring new challenges. This adventurous streak is a testament to his curious and fearless approach to life. Additionally, Powell has a creative side that extends beyond acting. He enjoys writing and often collaborates on projects that align with his artistic vision.

Whether brainstorming ideas for a script or contributing to the creative direction of a project, Powell's passion for storytelling is a recurring theme in both his professional and personal endeavors. At the core of Powell's personal life are his values and beliefs, which guide his decisions and interactions. He often emphasizes the importance of gratitude and staying humble, even amidst the pressures of fame. In interviews, Powell has spoken about his commitment to authenticity, both in his work and personal relationships. A staunch advocate for giving back, Powell frequently participates in charitable initiatives and supports causes close to his heart.

From environmental conservation efforts to educational programs, he uses his platform to make a positive impact on society. His philanthropic efforts reflect his belief in using his success to uplift others and contribute to meaningful change.

Balancing Fame and Privacy

Navigating the complexities of fame while maintaining a sense of normalcy can be challenging, but Powell has managed to strike a balance. He attributes much of this to his strong support system and his ability to stay grounded. By prioritizing meaningful relationships and setting boundaries, he ensures that his personal life remains a source of stability and joy. Powell's approach to fame is refreshingly down-to-earth. Rather than seeking constant attention, he focuses on building a fulfilling life that aligns with his values. This balanced perspective has not only helped him maintain his privacy but also earned him the respect of his peers and fans.

Insights into His Personality

Those who know Powell often describe him as charismatic, kind, and approachable. His sense of humor and ability to connect with people on a personal level make him a natural leader and collaborator. Whether on set or in social settings, Powell's infectious energy and genuine nature leave a lasting impression. Powell's optimistic outlook and drive for self-improvement are key aspects of his personality.

He approaches challenges with determination and views setbacks as opportunities to grow. This resilience, combined with his unwavering passion for his craft, has been instrumental in his success. As Powell continues to navigate his personal and professional life, his ability to stay true to himself remains a defining characteristic. His relationships, hobbies, and values all contribute to a life that is as rich and dynamic off-screen as it is on-screen. With his charisma and grounded nature, Powell serves as an inspiration to fans and aspiring artists alike. His personal journey is a testament to the power of staying authentic and embracing life's adventures, both big and small.

Chapter 6: Net Worth

Financial Success in Hollywood

Glen Powell's growing career in Hollywood has contributed significantly to his rising net worth. His ability to balance blockbuster roles, independent films, and creative pursuits such as writing and producing has positioned him as a versatile talent with multiple streams of income. As of recent estimates, Powell's net worth is reportedly in the range of $7–$10 million, a testament to his dedication and strategic career choices.

Powell's financial success stems largely from his acting career. With roles in commercially successful films like Hidden Figures and Top Gun: Maverick, he has earned lucrative paychecks and bonuses tied to box office performance. These high-profile projects not only brought him acclaim but also opened the door to more substantial earnings in subsequent films. In addition to his acting roles, Powell has also leveraged his celebrity status for brand endorsements and collaborations. Known for his impeccable style and charm, he has worked with leading fashion and lifestyle brands, further boosting his income.

Powell's association with brands often reflects his personality and interests. For instance, he has appeared in campaigns that highlight his adventurous spirit, such as collaborations with aviation or travel companies inspired by his role in Top Gun: Maverick. His ability to align himself with brands that resonate with his audience has made these partnerships mutually beneficial and highly lucrative.

Earnings as a Writer and Producer

Beyond acting, Powell's work as a writer and producer has become an important component of his financial portfolio. His involvement in projects like Set It Up showcased his ability to create and contribute to stories that connect with audiences. By taking on behind-the-scenes roles, Powell not only expands his creative influence but also earns a share of the profits as a producer. This dual role as an actor and producer is a strategic move that allows Powell to have greater control over his projects while securing additional revenue streams. His commitment to developing original content reflects his long-term vision for financial stability and creative fulfillment.

Like many successful actors, Powell has invested in real estate, which has become an integral part of his financial strategy. Known for his taste in architecture and design, he owns properties that reflect his appreciation for comfort and aesthetics. One notable purchase includes a modern home in Los Angeles, complete with state-of-the-art amenities and ample space for entertaining guests. This investment not only serves as a personal retreat but also as a valuable asset that continues to appreciate in value.

Powell's foray into real estate demonstrates his understanding of building wealth through diverse investments. Despite his growing net worth, Powell is committed to using his financial success for good. He actively supports various charitable causes, from educational initiatives to environmental conservation. His philanthropic efforts underscore his belief in giving back to the community and making a meaningful impact. Powell's approach to philanthropy is deeply personal. Rather than simply donating money, he often lends his time and influence to raise awareness for causes he is passionate about. This hands-on approach not only amplifies his contributions but also inspires others to follow his lead.

Powell's financial success is not just a result of his talent but also his disciplined approach to money management. In interviews, he has emphasized the importance of making thoughtful choices and planning for the future. Whether negotiating contracts or selecting investment opportunities, Powell approaches his finances with the same focus and determination that defines his career. One key aspect of his financial philosophy is diversification.

By building multiple income streams and investing in different sectors, Powell ensures long-term financial stability. This proactive approach allows him to pursue creative projects without compromising his financial security. As Powell's career continues to evolve, his net worth is expected to grow in tandem with his success. Upcoming projects, including acting roles and production ventures, promise to further solidify his position as a financially savvy entertainer. With a clear vision for his career and a commitment to making smart financial choices, Powell is well on his way to achieving lasting wealth. His journey serves as an example of how passion and pragmatism can work together to create a fulfilling and prosperous life.

Chapter 7: Legacy and Impact

Influence on the Film Industry

Glen Powell's contributions to Hollywood extend far beyond his on-screen performances. Through his versatility and dedication, Powell has become a respected figure in the entertainment industry, known for selecting roles that challenge conventional storytelling and push creative boundaries.

One of Powell's most notable impacts has been his ability to bridge the gap between traditional and contemporary cinema. From historical dramas like Hidden Figures to high-octane blockbusters like Top Gun: Maverick, Powell demonstrates an uncanny ability to adapt to diverse genres while maintaining authenticity. His talent for embodying characters with depth and relatability has made him a favorite among directors and audiences alike. Moreover, Powell's work as a writer and producer has added another dimension to his legacy. By contributing to the creative process behind the camera, he has influenced the direction and tone of projects, ensuring that his artistic vision resonates throughout.

His dual roles in films like Set It Up highlight his ability to create compelling narratives that capture the hearts of viewers. Powell's impact extends beyond the silver screen, as he actively engages in causes that matter to him. Through philanthropy and advocacy, he has used his platform to address social issues and inspire change. One of his most significant contributions has been promoting diversity and inclusion in Hollywood.

By participating in projects like Hidden Figures, which shed light on the untold stories of marginalized groups, Powell has championed representation in the industry. His commitment to supporting diverse narratives helps pave the way for a more inclusive future in film. Powell is also a vocal advocate for education and mentorship. Recognizing the importance of nurturing talent, he often works with aspiring filmmakers and actors, sharing his experiences and offering guidance. His efforts to uplift the next generation reflect his belief in the power of storytelling to shape perspectives and bring people together.

Recognition in Awards and Honors

While Glen Powell has yet to receive major individual awards, his work has garnered significant recognition within the industry. Films like Hidden Figures and Top Gun: Maverick have received numerous accolades, with Powell's performances often singled out as highlights.

For instance, Hidden Figures won the Screen Actors Guild Award for Outstanding Performance by a Cast in a Motion Picture, a testament to the collective strength of its ensemble cast, including Powell. Similarly, Top Gun: Maverick received widespread acclaim for its action sequences and storytelling, with Powell's role as "Hangman" earning praise from critics and fans alike. These achievements underscore Powell's ability to contribute meaningfully to collaborative efforts, earning him respect as a team player and a talented actor. As his career continues to flourish, he is likely to receive further recognition for his individual accomplishments. One of Powell's most enduring legacies is his ability to inspire aspiring artists and audiences worldwide.

His journey from a young boy with big dreams in Texas to a celebrated actor and producer in Hollywood serves as a powerful example of perseverance and passion. Through his work, Powell encourages others to embrace their uniqueness and pursue their goals relentlessly. His willingness to take on diverse roles and explore new creative avenues demonstrates the importance of adaptability and continuous growth. Fans often admire Powell not just for his talent but for his authenticity and kindness.

His interactions with fans, both online and in person, reflect a genuine appreciation for the support he receives. This connection further solidifies his status as a role model, reminding people that success is most meaningful when shared with others. At the heart of Glen Powell's legacy is his dedication to storytelling. Whether through acting, writing, or producing, he consistently seeks to tell stories that entertain, educate, and inspire. His ability to balance artistry with commercial success sets him apart as a true innovator in the industry. Powell's influence will likely be felt for years to come, as his work continues to resonate with audiences and shape the cinematic landscape.

By championing stories that matter and staying true to his creative vision, he ensures that his contributions to Hollywood are both impactful and enduring.

Looking to the Future

As Powell's career evolves, his legacy is still being written. With upcoming projects that promise to showcase his range and talent, he remains a force to be reckoned with in the entertainment world. His dedication to excellence and his commitment to making a difference ensure that his impact will only continue to grow. Whether as an actor, a producer, or a philanthropist, Glen Powell's journey is a testament to the power of determination and creativity. His legacy is not just one of success but one of inspiration, reminding us all of the transformative power of storytelling.

Chapter 8: Professional Skills

Mastery of Acting

Glen Powell's acting skills are the foundation of his success and have set him apart in an industry teeming with talent. Known for his versatility, Powell has seamlessly transitioned between genres, from historical dramas like Hidden Figures to action-packed blockbusters like Top Gun: Maverick. His ability to embody diverse characters with authenticity and depth reflects years of dedication to honing his craft.

Powell's performances are characterized by his keen emotional intelligence, allowing him to connect deeply with the roles he portrays. He has a unique talent for balancing charm and vulnerability, making his characters relatable and multidimensional. Whether playing the cocky yet lovable "Hangman" in Top Gun: Maverick or the earnest astronaut John Glenn in Hidden Figures, Powell brings nuance to every performance, leaving a lasting impression on audiences. Another aspect of Powell's acting skill is his physicality. He approaches physically demanding roles with discipline and precision, often undergoing rigorous training to bring authenticity to his performances.

For Top Gun: Maverick, he not only mastered the technical aspects of aviation but also maintained a rigorous fitness routine to meet the role's physical demands. This dedication underscores his commitment to delivering performances that are both believable and engaging.

Talent as a Writer

Beyond acting, Glen Powell has showcased his talent as a writer, contributing to projects that reflect his creative vision. His work on romantic comedies, such as Set It Up, reveals his ability to craft engaging and witty narratives that resonate with audiences. Powell's writing often blends humor and heart, creating stories that are both entertaining and meaningful. As a writer, Powell draws inspiration from his own experiences and observations, infusing his scripts with authenticity and relatability. His collaborative approach to writing ensures that the final product benefits from diverse perspectives, resulting in well-rounded and compelling storytelling.

Powell's writing also demonstrates his understanding of pacing and character development. He creates dynamic arcs for his characters, ensuring that their journeys feel organic and satisfying. This attention to detail has earned him praise not only as a performer but also as a storyteller with a distinctive voice. Powell's skills as a producer further highlight his multifaceted abilities.

By taking on production roles, he has gained greater control over the creative process, allowing him to bring his unique vision to life. His work as a producer emphasizes collaboration and innovation, ensuring that each project aligns with his artistic values. Producing requires a blend of creativity and business acumen, and Powell excels in both areas. He has a keen eye for identifying compelling stories and assembling talented teams to execute them. From securing funding to overseeing post-production, Powell is actively involved in every stage of the filmmaking process, demonstrating his versatility and leadership.

Powell's production ventures also reflect his commitment to nurturing fresh talent. By championing emerging writers, directors, and actors, he helps bring new voices to the forefront of Hollywood. This dedication to fostering creativity underscores his desire to contribute meaningfully to the industry's evolution. A defining trait of Powell's professional skills is his ability to collaborate effectively.

On set, he is known for fostering a positive and inclusive atmosphere, earning the respect of his colleagues. His charisma and approachability make him a natural leader, while his willingness to listen and adapt ensures that every team member feels valued. Powell's collaborative spirit extends beyond his work with cast and crew. In his writing and producing endeavors, he actively seeks input from others, recognizing the importance of diverse perspectives in creating impactful stories. This openness to collaboration has been instrumental in his success, as it allows him to build strong professional relationships and produce high-quality work. One of Powell's greatest professional strengths is his adaptability.

In an industry that is constantly evolving, he has demonstrated an impressive ability to embrace change and take on new challenges. Whether exploring different genres, learning new skills for a role, or stepping into unfamiliar territory as a producer, Powell approaches each opportunity with enthusiasm and determination. His growth mindset is evident in his career trajectory.

Powell continuously seeks ways to improve his craft and expand his skill set, ensuring that he remains relevant and competitive in the ever-changing landscape of Hollywood. This dedication to self-improvement has not only contributed to his success but also inspired others in the industry to strive for excellence. Powell's professional skills extend beyond his technical abilities to include his unwavering professionalism. He is known for his work ethic, reliability, and commitment to delivering his best, both on and off the screen. These qualities have earned him the admiration of his peers and established him as a trusted collaborator in the industry.

By combining talent, creativity, and professionalism, Powell has built a reputation as a multifaceted artist who consistently delivers exceptional work. His dedication to his craft and his willingness to push boundaries ensure that his contributions to Hollywood will continue to be celebrated for years to come.

The Future of Powell's Career

As Glen Powell continues to evolve as an actor, writer, and producer, his professional skills will undoubtedly play a key role in shaping his future. With his ability to adapt, innovate, and collaborate, he is poised to take on even greater challenges and achieve new heights in his career. Whether exploring uncharted genres, creating groundbreaking content, or mentoring the next generation of talent, Powell's professional journey is one of growth and ambition. His skills not only define his success but also set the stage for an enduring legacy in Hollywood.

Conclusion

Glen Powell's journey through Hollywood has been marked by steady growth, diversification, and an unwavering commitment to his craft. From his humble beginnings in Texas to becoming one of the most sought-after actors in the industry, Powell has proven that talent, perseverance, and authenticity are key ingredients for long-term success.

As an actor, writer, and producer, Powell has managed to carve a niche for himself in a competitive industry. His early roles might have been overlooked by many, but Powell's ability to take on diverse and challenging characters catapulted him to prominence. Films like Hidden Figures showcased his range as an actor, while Top Gun: Maverick solidified him as a leading man capable of carrying major franchises. With each role, Powell not only earned the respect of audiences but also that of critics and industry insiders. Yet, it is not only his acting that has defined his career.

Powell's ventures into writing and producing have added a new dimension to his professional portfolio, allowing him to shape the stories that are told on screen. His work in Set It Up demonstrated his ability to bring humor and heart to romantic comedies, while his behind-the-scenes contributions to other films reflect his broader vision for Hollywood storytelling. Powell's influence in Hollywood goes beyond his acting and producing skills.

His advocacy for diversity, inclusion, and representation in film is a crucial part of his legacy. By participating in projects that highlight marginalized voices and stories, such as Hidden Figures, Powell has helped to reshape the landscape of modern cinema. His belief in storytelling as a means of fostering empathy and understanding ensures that his impact will continue to be felt for generations to come. As an advocate for the next generation of filmmakers, Powell's efforts to mentor young talent reflect his commitment to creating a sustainable and inclusive entertainment industry.

He actively supports initiatives that empower aspiring creators, providing a platform for them to showcase their voices. This dedication to mentorship has earned him admiration not just as an entertainer, but as a leader in the industry who seeks to elevate others along the way. Looking to the future, Glen Powell's trajectory appears even brighter. With several exciting projects on the horizon, he is poised to further establish himself as a top-tier talent.

Whether stepping into new genres, taking on challenging new roles, or expanding his influence behind the camera, Powell's future in Hollywood is filled with boundless potential. His versatility will continue to be an asset as he navigates an industry that constantly evolves. Powell has already shown that he is not afraid to take risks, whether by stepping outside his comfort zone to tackle more serious roles or diving into producing and writing. This adaptability will ensure that his career remains dynamic and relevant, as he continues to push boundaries and grow as a multifaceted artist. In many ways, Glen Powell's story is a testament to the power of perseverance and self-belief.

He has worked hard to build a successful career, overcoming challenges and continuously striving for improvement. His journey serves as an inspiration to others who aspire to make their mark in Hollywood, proving that success comes not just from raw talent but from a combination of hard work, patience, and passion. Moreover, Powell's down-to-earth personality and commitment to his values make him a relatable figure for many.

His ability to stay grounded amidst the pressures of fame reflects the strength of his character. Whether interacting with fans, collaborating with colleagues, or pursuing personal interests, Powell remains true to himself—an admirable trait in an industry often driven by external expectations. Glen Powell's legacy will undoubtedly endure, not only because of his professional achievements but also because of the positive impact he has made on the film industry and society as a whole. His future is filled with promise, and as he continues to evolve, so too will the mark he leaves on the world. Glen Powell is more than just a talented actor; he is a storyteller, a producer, and a leader in Hollywood.

His journey reflects the evolution of an artist who continuously pushes himself to grow, adapt, and inspire. From his breakout roles to his work behind the scenes, Powell has proven time and again that he is a force to be reckoned with in the entertainment industry. As Powell's career continues to flourish, his impact will undoubtedly grow. He has laid the foundation for a legacy that will inspire future generations of artists, entertainers, and creators. The next chapter of his journey is just beginning, and if his past success is any indication, it promises to be as exciting and influential as what has come before.

www.ingramcontent.com/pod-product-compliance
Lightning Source LLC
Chambersburg PA
CBHW070940220526
45469CB00007B/2455